THE WONDERFUL WORLD
OF NETSUKE

PLATE 2. **HAIRY AINU.** The Ainu are the aborigines of Japan. According to their oral legends, they came from a land of snow and ice devoid of forests or birds. The land of their legends is thought to be Siberia. They are a Caucasian race, taller and bonier than the Japanese, with luxuriant mustaches and beards as opposed to the smooth-skinned Japanese. Originally the Ainu were settled extensively throughout Japan, but today they are concentrated around Shiraoi in Hokkaido, the northern Japanese island, in much the same way as the American Indians on the Arizona reservations.

The Ainu's life is one of fishing and hunting. The great annual Ainu festival is devoted to the worship and sacrifice of a bear. In the illustration, the Ainu is carrying a catch of seals on his back.

The geometric patterns on Ainu clothes resemble American Indian decorations. Like the Scotsman's plaid, the pattern tells which village or clan an Ainu traveler is from. Material: wood. Unsigned. Height: 7.9 cm. From the collection of Cornelius Van S. Roosevelt, Washington, D. C.

The Wonderful World of Netsuke

With One Hundred
Masterpieces of Miniature Sculpture in Color

by RAYMOND BUSHELL

CHARLES E. TUTTLE CO., INC.

Rutland, Vermont   Tokyo, Japan

Representatives
Continental Europe: BOXERBOOKS, INC., Zurich
British Isles: PRENTICE-HALL INTERNATIONAL, INC., London
Australasia: PAUL FLESCH & CO., PTY. LTD., Melbourne

Published by the Charles E. Tuttle Company, Inc.
of Rutland, Vermont & Tokyo, Japan
with editorial offices at
Suido, 1-chome, 2–6, Bunkyo-ku, Tokyo, Japan

Library of Congress Catalog Card No. 64–24948
First edition, 1964

PRINTED IN JAPAN

TABLE OF CONTENTS

LIST OF ILLUSTRATIONS

INTRODUCTION

The Japanese love of the miniature in art is well known—dwarf trees, tray landscapes, sword fittings, and woodblock prints. Miniature sculpture of figures, masks, dolls, and Buddhist images has played an important role in Japanese daily life since ancient times. During the Tokugawa and Meiji periods (1603–1912), miniature sculpture of a special type was born. It is called *netsuke*.

Netsuke are carvings of ivory, wood, lacquer, porcelain, metal, or other material. They are generally about 4 centimeters ($1\frac{1}{2}$ inches) in size, but vary between 2 centimeters (4/5 inch) and 9 centimeters ($3\frac{1}{2}$ inches) or larger.

For some 300 years, every well-dressed Japanese wore at the sash of his kimono a netsuke as an attachment to his purse, pouch, or lacquer box. It is the use of the netsuke as an article to be *worn* that distinguishes it from other miniature sculpture. To be suitable for wearing, it had to be even smaller than most miniature sculpture, it had to be rounded and smooth, and it had to have a passage for the cord that attached it to the purse, pouch, or lacquer box. The netsuke artist worked under these requirements that did not burden other sculptors.

In its shadowy beginnings, the netsuke served as an article of utility; but the Japanese artistic genius does not permit objects of common use to go unimproved. The netsuke progressed through stages of shaping, carving, and decorating into an object of show and vanity, much as the jeweled ring of today. Every technique of the sculptor's craft was employed, from relief, high, low, etched, or sunken, to full round figures and groups; and every style, from microscopic ornateness to monumental simplicity. Most fine netsuke are carved from solid blocks of choice material, and some are enhanced by the addition of color or inlay.

There are few more pleasant ways of becoming acquainted with the Japanese than through an examination of a comprehensive netsuke collection. They reveal a great deal of Japanese life that is not found in the history books. Netsuke was a popular art, and the subject matter was unlimited. History and legend; gods and saints; ghosts and goblins; animals, real and fanciful; people of all stations, callings, and conditions; habits and customs, quaint, surprising, and lusty; activities, innocent, spiritual, earthy, and naughty; all are the domain of the irrepressible netsuke artists.

Less than half of all netsuke are signed. The early ones are usually not signed. Our knowledge of the artists is very scanty, and almost nothing is known of the various carving schools. Source, provenance, and pedigree hardly exist—except for the records of a few English collections dating from this century. Therein, paradoxically, lies one of the great charms of netsuke as an art form. Our delight and appreciation tend to spring from their intrinsic artistic merit rather than from less valid considerations of signature, artist, school, attribution, provenance, and pedigree.

One of the most appealing qualities of a netsuke is a quality that, amazingly, was not carved into it by the artist who created it. It is the smoothness and lustre brought about by successive generations of loving handling and wearing. It is the *owner's* contribution to the netsuke. The Japanese call this quality *aji*. A netsuke without *aji* is somehow incomplete.

Netsuke are no longer in common use—the introduction of Western dress contributed to their demise—but they are more alive today than ever before. They are established throughout the world as collectors' items, prized examples of the fine art of miniature sculpture.

ACKNOWLEDGMENTS

I am greatly indebted to Mr. Katsuya Yanagihara, Mr. Kazuo Itoh, and Mr. Shohei Uchino for their reliable readings and translations.

Mr. Kenzo Imai of Kyoto is an expert judge of netsuke and elucidated many recondite meanings.

The many collectors who generously loaned me their netsuke for photographing are identified in the captions to the illustrations. Their names appear preceded by the phrase, "From the collection of . . ." Wherever possible, I have also indicated the person or shop from which the illustrated netsuke was purchased.

I am especially grateful to Mr. Zenshiro Horie of Nagoya and to

Mr. Yonekichi Matsui of Osaka, whose generosity and helpfulness were so unbounded that they placed their wonderful collections at my complete disposal.

Miss Mayko Tanaka helped far beyond the duties of even a most conscientious secretary. Very often her services were performed in secret and discovered only by accident.

NOTE

I am delighted to correspond on all aspects of netsuke. Letters addressed to the publisher will reach me.

Tokyo, Japan   Raymond Bushell

PLATE 3. **CURLY-HAIRED EUROPEAN.** The first Europeans to visit Japan were Portuguese sailors who drifted ashore in 1543. Portuguese and Dutch merchants were permitted to settle at Deshima, a small island in Nagasaki harbor, but their trading activities were severely limited and their movements restricted to the island. Even these small privileges were cancelled in the early 17th century when the clannish Japanese adopted a policy of strict isolation.

Strange clothes, curly hair, blue eyes, and long noses were some of the features of the first Portuguese and Dutch settlers that astounded the Japanese. Material: mother-of-pearl. Unsigned. Height: 6.8 cm. Formerly in the collection of Baron Masuda. From the collection of B. K. Denton, St. Louis. For other Europeans, see Plates 4, 5, and 6.

PLATE 4. **EUROPEANS WITH DOGS.** Europeans holding dogs, cocks, and monkeys were frequently portrayed in netsuke. These animals are native to Japan, but the European breeds, like the dogs in the illustrations, were new and remarkable, and so had great popular appeal in painting and sculpture.

Left: Material: ivory. Unsigned. Height: 12 cm. From the collection of Elizabeth Humphreys-Owen, London.

Right: Material: ivory. Unsigned. Height: 10 cm. From the collection of Frances Numano, Tokyo.

For other Europeans, see Plates 3, 5, and 6.

PLATE 5. **EUROPEAN AND GAME.** Firearms and spyglasses were some of the instruments, and cockfighting and hunting were some of the diversions of the Europeans that the Japanese artists portrayed. Material: ivory. Unsigned. Height: 12 cm. From Masao Morita, Kyoto. For other Europeans, see Plates 3, 4, and 6.

PLATE 6. **FANCIFUL EUROPEANS.** Some of the earlier representations of Europeans, as in the illustrations, are extremely fanciful. It is likely that the sculptor never saw a European in the flesh but compounded distortions by using as models the paintings and carvings of other Japanese—or possibly by relying on wild descriptions and reports.

Clothes are the surest criteria for distinguishing Dutchmen from Portuguese, just as in the case of Japanese and Chinese. The Dutch are portrayed with long coats and conical or curled hats and the Portuguese with balloon-shaped pantaloons and stiff brimmed hats.

Left: Material: wood. Unsigned. Height: 11.4 cm. From K. Yamada, Tokyo.
Right: Material: ivory. Unsigned. Height: 9 cm. From Z. Izuoka, Kyoto.
For other Europeans, see Plates 3, 4, and 5.

PLATE 7. **MONKEY SONGOKU.** Priest Sanzo, before returning to China, spent many years in India collecting Buddhist relics and books in fulfillment of a vow.

He was ably assisted by Songoku, a monkey of great magical powers. Sanzo was required to perform 108 difficult feats of holiness. Monkey Songoku plucked 108 hairs from his body and blew them into 108 replicas of his master. The 108 Sanzos thus created easily performed one feat each.

In the illustration, Songoku carries his magic wand and the sacred books and scrolls which he secured in India. The figure has 108 delicate inlays of pearl, coral, jade, and other semi-precious stones. No doubt each stone stands for one of the 108 feats of holiness that Sanzo performed. One hundred and eight is a magic number in Buddhist lore. The Buddhist rosary contains 108 beads; the Buddhist bell has 108 nipples; and at New Year's the gong sounds 108 times. Material: wood with various inlays. Unsigned. Height: 9.3 cm. From the collection of Cornelius Van S. Roosevelt, Washington, D.C. For other Monkeys, see Plates 59 and 60.

PLATE 8. **KUDAN.** Interesting sources of subject matter for the netsuke artists were the wildly imaginative drawings of unreal men and beasts found in ancient Chinese books. The animal illustrated is a *kudan*. It has the body of a bull with a bearded human head, three supplementary eyes on either side of its body, and horns.

The kudan is an oracle with a human voice which always utters the absolute truth. In view of the kudan's European face and the fame of the Delphic oracle, Greek influence or a Greek model may well be presumed. Material: ivory. Unsigned. Length: 4.9 cm. From the collection of Cornelius Van S. Roosevelt, Washington, D.C.

19

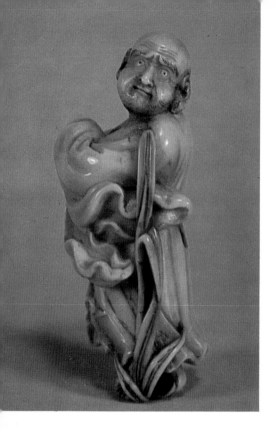

PLATE 9. **DARUMA AS SAINT.** Daruma is credited with founding the Zen sect of Buddhism and with bringing Zen to Japan. Zen is sometimes defined as a system for training the mind and body by meditation. Tea drinking is also ascribed to Daruma, as he found the practice helpful in maintaining wakefulness during prolonged meditations.

Daruma is represented supported by a single reed as a gentle wind wafts him across a body of water. According to Chinese legend, the body of water was the Yangtze River, which Daruma crossed on his way to a missionary center; according to Japanese legend, it was the sea on his voyage from China to Japan.

Chinese artists treat Daruma with reverence, whereas Japanese artists often portray him as a ludicrous figure. The expression of suffering virtue and saintly patience exhibited by Daruma in the illustration seems more facetious than reverent. Material: ivory. Signed: Hidetsune. Height: 4.8 cm. From the collection of U. A. Casal. Kobe. For other Darumas, see Plates 11 and 12.

PLATE 10. **MERMAID AND CHILD.** The mermaid legend may have originated from wishful reports of love-starved seamen about the sea cow, an aquatic relative of the elephant, that feeds on seaweed in shallow waters. Being a mammal, it nurses its young at the breast just as the mermaid is doing in the illustration.

The mermaid is called *ningyo* in Japanese, meaning woman-fish. Alas, the complaint against this beautiful creature is that she is not enough fish to eat nor enough woman to love! Material: wood. Signed: Kokei. Length: 4.7 cm. From the collection of Yonekichi Matsui, Osaka.

PLATE 11. **WOMAN DARUMA.** Daruma in roly-poly form is sometimes carved with a woman's features. In the illustration, the face is that of Otafuku, the storied homely, good-natured, and talkative woman. Daruma and Otafuku strike the Japanese funny bone equally as laughable figures—in combination they are irresistible.

The Woman Daruma is a ridicule of the idea that a woman can keep her tongue quiet as required for long periods of meditation. Material: lacquered wood. Signed: Meizan. Height: 3.1 cm. From K. Yamada, Tokyo. For other Darumas, see Plates 9 and 12.

PLATE 12. **DARUMA AS TOY.** Daruma is the Buddhist saint who faced the wall in solitary meditation for nine years until his legs wasted away. The Japanese carvers treat Daruma with jocular humor. He is the roly-poly of Japan, always returning upright no matter how often he is tumbled, an allusion to his atrophied legs as well as to his patience. The Japanese have a common expression for the undaunted spirit which comes from Daruma: Seven times down, eight times up.

Ladies of the night are often mistakenly or euphemistically referred to by foreigners as geisha. Their Japanese friends humorously refer to these ladies as "Daruma geisha." Material: boxwood face, teak body, and ebony base. Signed: Segai. Height: 2.8 cm. From the collection of Abram Gercik, Vancouver. For other Darumas, see Plates 9 and 11.

Plate 13. **WILD BOAR.** In the Orient the boar is considered the most courageous of all wild beasts because it hurls itself straight at its enemy with single-minded concentration. It looks neither right nor left, giving no thought to retreat. It is always dangerous and very hard to kill.

The introduction of Buddhism into Japan brought with it a revulsion to the eating of meat. With characteristic logic, butchers counteracted the qualms of customers by renaming the boar "the mountain whale" *(yama kujira)*, a term still in use. As fish, the Buddhist prohibitions did not apply, and those who liked boar meat could gorge themselves, completely free of ulcerating misgivings. Material: wood. Signed: Masatomo. Length: 4.4 cm. From the collection of Mrs. Kenneth Hall, Montreal. For another Boar, see Plate 14.

Plate 14. **WILD BOAR GROUP.** The Chinese concept of dualism as a basic principle of nature and of the universe greatly influenced Japanese philosophy and art. The illustration represents the dual principle; male and female, sleeping and awake, up and down, active and passive, direction and counterdirection, etc. Material: wood. Signed: Tomokazu. Length: 5.1 cm. From the collection of Abram Gercik, Vancouver. For another Boar, see Plate 13.

PLATE 15. **HORSE AND MARE.** The horse has figured prominently in Japanese history since time immemorial. In early barbaric times important possessions, horses, and servants were buried alive with deceased royalty. Later, clay figures of horses and servants were buried as substitutes for their living counterparts. These clay figures are known as *haniwa*.

In former times many shrines kept a sacred white horse. It was worshipped as a symbol in the ancient Shinto ritual of confession and purification. At many shrine festivals, horses are meticulously groomed, beautifully bridled, adorned with colored and gold ornaments, and led by anciently attired attendants at the head of the processions.

Wealthy worshippers acquired merit by donating sacred horses to the shrine. The common people who could not afford live horses gave paintings of horses instead. The horses were painted on framed five-sided wooden tablets known as *ema*. Originally all ema paintings were of horses, but later many other subjects were added. A special technique of ema painting developed, and now fine ema paintings are collectors' items. Material: ivory. Unsigned. Height: 5.1 cm. From Kikutaro Tsuruta, Tokyo. Illustrated in *Horses in Japan* by Vivienne Kenrick. For other Horses, see Plates 16, 17, and 18.

PLATE 16. **RESTING HORSE.** The horse moves proudly in many stirring episodes of Japanese history and legend:

Oguri Hangan subdued a vicious stallion until he made it stand with all four legs on a wooden chess board.

Gentoku escaped an ambush by mounting his horse and leaping 30 feet across a river flooding a deep ravine to the safety of the opposite bank.

Taketsuna and Kagesue, on borrowed horses, raced across the Uji River in the face of a storm of arrows in order to be first to meet the enemy.

Narihira, Japan's Don Juan and one of its Six Great Poets, rode into exile after a romantic intrigue with the empress.

Yoshitsune, on his famous black steed, rode almost straight down a mountainside in order to attack the enemy in the rear. Material: ivory. Signed: Gyokutosai. Length: 4.6 cm. From the collection of Mrs. Kenneth Hall, Montreal. For other Horses, see Plates 15, 17, and 18.

PLATE 17. **HORSE AND RAT.** The rat is the first year and the horse the seventh year of the 12-year zodiac calendar. The seventh year after one's birth year is considered lucky. Many Japanese born in the Year of the Rat will anticipate good fortune in the Year of the Horse because of the separation by the lucky number seven.

However, women so unfortunate as to be born in the Year of the Horse, Cycle of Fire, known as the Fire Horse Year, are allegorically considered husband-devourers, and marriage for them is difficult to arrange, especially in country districts. The popular superstition is that husbands married to women born in the Fire Horse Year are fated to die young. Fortunately the Fire Horse Year occurs only once every 60 years. Material: wood. Signed: Tomokazu. Length: 4.6 cm. From Tokuo Inami, Tokyo. For other Horses, see Plates 15, 16, and 18.

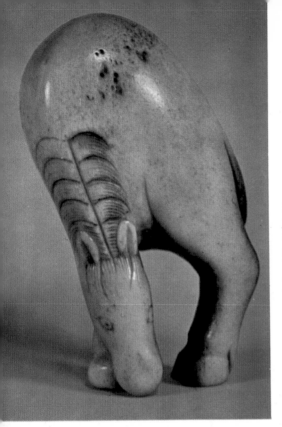

PLATE 18. **STANDING HORSE.** When a Japanese says that he is a horse, he does not mean that he is about to gallop away on four legs. He means that he was born in the Year of the Horse. With a little simple arithmetic, another Japanese who knows the fixed order of the twelve Zodiac animals will know how old he is, based on the fact that the Year of the Horse occurs every 12th year. For example, the man who says he is a horse is 12, 24, 36, 48, etc. during the Year of the Horse. Material: staghorn. Unsigned. Height: 5.8 cm. From Yamasada, Kyoto. For other Horses, see Plates 15, 16, and 17.

PLATE 19. **RAKAN.** *Rakan* are Buddhist saints who have completely freed themselves of all earthly desires and possessions. They are the original disciples of Buddha and number 500.

There are many temples in Japan containing statues of the Five Hundred Rakan. Each rakan has distinctive features, expression, and physique. The belief is that one will find the person for whom one seeks among the numerous faces of the Five Hundred Rakan.

In Kawagoe, a person seeking a loved one or a sweetheart goes to the Kita-in Temple on a dark, moonless night and touches the features of each rakan successively until he finds one that is warm to his touch. He identifies the warm rakan by sticking a piece of paper to it. The next day, according to the local belief, he will find his lost relation or sweetheart in the features of the warm rakan. Material: black pottery with gold details. Signed: Mokubei. Height: 5 cm. From the collection of Jacob Tropp, Tokyo.

PLATE 20. **HANDAKA SONJA.** Handaka Sonja is one of the Sixteen Apostles of Buddha. The attributes of the Apostles are long drooping eyebrows, enlarged pendulous earlobes denoting great wisdom, a shaved head with well-marked cranial areas, and a countenance of intense spiritual concentration. The Apostle usually wears a single garment clasped at one shoulder, with the other shoulder bare. Handaka Sonja is distinguished by a companion dragon which sometimes lies at his feet like a faithful dog, as in the illustration.

The carving is attributed to Yoshimura Shuzan, the greatest of all netsuke artists. Shuzan never signed his work. The mellowness of the colors, the originality of the design, and particularly the power of the carving indicate authenticity. Material: painted wood. Unsigned. Attributed to Yoshimura Shuzan. Height: 9.2 cm. From Kyushiro Honma, Tokyo.

PLATE 21. **OWL.** The Chinese and, through their early influence, the Japanese regard the owl as a thoroughly evil bird. Not only is it a nocturnal predator, its call a portent of death and an alert to snatch the departing soul, but, worst of all, it eats its own mother. This is a most unfilial act in a filially devoted society where patricide is punished more dreadfully than ordinary murder.

It is no surprise then that the owl was seldom carved. Who would want to wear an omen of evil and a symbol of ingratitude? As a netsuke it is a rare bird, and the collector is always searching for a good one. Material: wood. Unsigned. Height: 5 cm. From the collection of Abram Gercik, Vancouver.

PLATE 22. **MOUNT FUJI AND PLOVERS.** A familiar theme of the Japanese landscape painter is Mt. Fuji in the distance, pine trees in the middle ground, and plovers skimming the ocean waves in the foreground. Here, the netsuke artist has abbreviated the landscape to Mt. Fuji and plovers.

The plover is called *chidori* in Japanese, which means "thousand birds." The picturesque name derives from the birds, traveling in large formations along the ocean shores, skimming and dipping in rhythm with the waves. Material: true pearl and gold. Signed: Ichigyoku. Length: 3.8 cm. From Azuma Brothers, Tokyo. From the collection of Frances Numano, Tokyo.

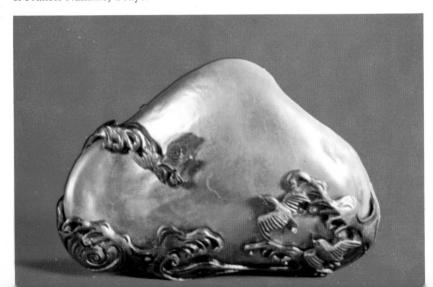

PLATE 23. **BUSHO KILLING THE TIGER.** Busho is one of a band of brigands who terrorized a part of China in the 13th century. The brigands' evil exploits were aggrandized in a novel, *The Hundred and Eight Heroes of China,* which contains about the same proportion of truth, distortion, and legend as *Robin Hood and His Merry Men.* The novel was translated into Japanese in 1806 with the title *Suikoden* and profusely illustrated by the prolific and imaginative Hokusai and by the blood-dripping brush of Toyokuni.

The exploit represented here is Busho holding a tiger down with his foot and killing it with a single blow of his fist. Material: ivory. Signed: Minkoku. Height: 3.6 cm. From Kazuo Itoh, Tokyo.

PLATE 24. **JAVANESE SWORD HANDLE.** In the early days of netsuke, articles originating in China, Indonesia, Thailand, and Oceania were sometimes transformed into netsuke by the addition of holes for attachment. It is often difficult to determine whether a netsuke is a foreign article adapted for use as a netsuke or a foreign design imitated by a Japanese carver.

The article illustrated represents a Javanese sword handle in a traditional rendition of Ganesha, the elephant-headed god of India. Material: wood. Unsigned. Height: 6.4 cm. From Toraya, Tokyo. For other Foreign Designs, see Plates 51, 57, and 95.

PLATE 25. **GHOST.** Ghosts play a thrilling part in Japanese literature and drama. In stories, many a conscienceless murderer has been driven to his death by the incessant haunting of the ghost of his victim. Ghost plays are popular in the Kabuki theater, where they are usually performed in the hot summer months. The effects of ghostly make-up and unearthly screams keep the audience in blood-running coolness despite the stifling heat. Japanese ghosts are always portrayed without legs. Material: wood. Unsigned. Height: 8.2 cm. From Sukeichi Kaneko, Yokohama. For other Ghosts, Goblins, and Cadavers, see Plates 26, 27, and 28.

PLATE 26. **GHOST AND GOBLIN.** The representation is a travesty on mother and child. Mother is a ghost, and child is a goblin *(bakemono)*. Is mother going to nurse the little darling, or is she going to fix him for *her* supper?

In Japan, ghosts are ethereal, their extremities trailing off in legless appendages; bakemono are goblins and monsters of various terrifying shapes and sizes. The little fellow resembles the goblin known as Priest One-Eye, who travels about carrying fire in a sieve.

Many famous artists have tried their hand at painting One Hundred Ghosts or One Hundred Goblins. Should one take the trouble to count, one finds considerably fewer than 100, the number being used in the sense of "a great many." Material: wood. Signed: Masatoshi. Height: 6.5 cm. From Yonemasa, Tokyo. For other Ghosts and Cadavers, see Plates 25, 27, and 28.

PLATE 27. **NITTA YOSHISADA.** Nitta Yoshisada was one of the great generals who fought on the side of the emperor against the forces of the shogun during the civil wars of the Ashikaga period. At the battle of Fujishima (A.D. 1300), he was shot in the head by an enemy arrow. His head was severed, taken to Kyoto, and exhibited for public gaze. His devoted wife, who was to meet him in Kyoto after the battle, found instead this ghastly, grisly trophy hanging by the topknot. The bereaved woman retired to a convent and was never heard of again, but both her sons followed in their famous father's footsteps and, like him, were slaughtered in battle. Material: painted wood. Unsigned. Height: 4.7 cm. From the collection of Michael Braun, New York. For other Ghosts, Goblins, and Cadavers, see Plates 25, 26, and 28.

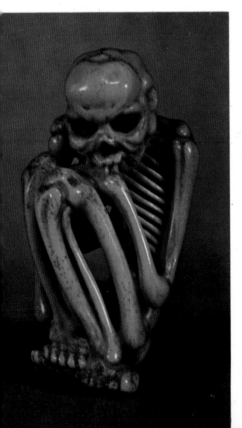

PLATE 28. **SKELETON.** The custom of cremating the dead is prevalent in Japan; only the ashes are interred. However, there was a time when the burial of the corpse was common. In accordance with Buddhist custom, the corpse was placed in a small square box in a cramped squatting position with the head bent towards the knees, as in the illustration. The position is thought to represent a final religious meditation, or a return to the foetal position preparatory to a rebirth.

The skeleton is a fine example of the solution of the netsuke carver's problem of how to design a dangling, *bony* object so that it is smooth and rounded for the ideal netsuke shape. Material: ivory. Unsigned. Height: 4.6 cm. From Joseph Seo, New York. Illustrated in *The Netsuke Handbook of Ueda Reikichi* (No. 64), adapted from the Japanese by Raymond Bushell. For other Ghosts, Goblins, and Cadavers, see Plates 25, 26, and 27.

PLATE 29. **BUTTERFLY.** The butterfly is the symbol of conjugal happiness. At wedding ceremonies saké bottles or teapots are often decorated with pairs of male and female butterflies as emblems of a happy union. Lovers in poems and novels sometimes express the wish to be reborn as butterflies.

One of the court dances is the Butterfly Dance *(Kocho no Mai)*. It is performed by six young ladies made up as butterflies and wearing wings attached to their shoulders. Material: ivory. Unsigned. Width: 5.2 cm. From Uchida Woodblock Print, Tokyo.

PLATE 30. **CHRISTIAN NETSUKE.** The closed metal box has an "innocent" Oriental design of dragons but opens to reveal a Christ on the Cross. The Japanese Christians suffered persecution and even massacre during the Tokugawa period. Consequently, they developed the practice of disguising their beliefs by nominal attendance at Buddhist and Shinto Shrines, of conducting services in secret, and of concealing the symbols of their faith.

The Japanese Christians around Nagasaki are known to this day as the Hiding Christians *(Kakure-Kirishitan)*. Material: metal and metal inlays. Unsigned. Length (open): 6.7 cm. From Kenzo Negishi, Tokyo. Illustrated in *Japan: A History in Art* by Bradley Smith.

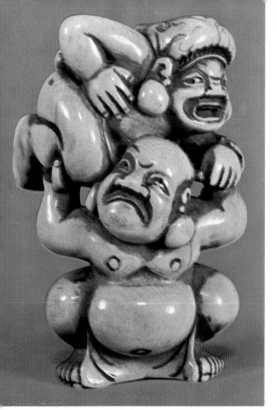

PLATE 31. **DAIKOKU AND EBISU WRESTLING.** Daikoku and Ebisu are two of the Seven Happy Gods of Japan. They represent prosperity. Daikoku's emblem is the rice bag, symbolizing the wealth of the land; Ebisu's emblem is the sea bream, symbolizing the wealth of the sea.

Ebisu and Daikoku preside over the New Year's festivities. In the illustration, they enter into the spirit of the occasion with a friendly wrestling match. Material: ivory. Unsigned. Height: 5.7 cm. From Shoji Sakai, Niigata.

PLATE 32. **KARAKO AT PLAY.** *Karako* (literally Chinese children) bear the same relationship to the religious arts of China and Japan as the cherubs and seraphs do to the religious arts of Christianity. There is one important difference: karako are not angelic children with wings; they are lusty, mischievous pranksters busy with games and acrobatics as in the illustration. In paintings, they are often portrayed at their duties of serving tea, carrying relics, and running errands for the great Taoists and Confucianists. Material: ivory. Unsigned. Height: 4.5 cm. From the collection of Yoshimatsu Tsuruki, Kyoto. Illustrated in *Yokei* (Happy Remainders) by Yoshimatsu Tsuruki. For another Karako, see Plate 33.

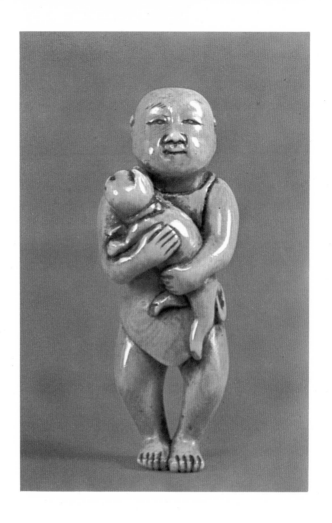

PLATE 33. **KARAKO HOLDING CAT.** Japanese netsuke carvers were very fond of the subject of Chinese children *(karako)*. They portrayed karako at various pranks, activities, and acrobatics, and at play with various animals as well as among themselves. The face of the little boy illustrated is pure Chinese. Material: ivory. Unsigned. Height: 5.6 cm. From the collection of Zenshiro Horie, Nagoya. For another Karako, see Plate 32.

PLATE 34. **DOG.** Among the native breeds of dogs are the Akita and the Tosa. In former times dogs were bred for fighting, and dog fighting was a popular sport. Even today dog fighting is occasionally conducted surreptitiously in some country districts. The Tosa is known as the strongest and most vicious of the fighting dogs.

There are three temples in Tokyo devoted exclusively to dogs and cats, one of them being the Saishin-ji Temple. The grounds contain over 40,000 stupas commemorating departed pets. Just as in the case of humans, the temple conducts a burial ceremony according to the Buddhist faith, bestows a posthumous religious name, and from time to time holds memorial services. Material: rhinoceros horn. Unsigned. Height: 5 cm. From the collection of Frances Numano, Tokyo. For another Dog, see Plate 36.

PLATE 35. **GIRAFFE GROUP.** The giraffe is called *kirin* in Japanese, the same word as is applied to the imaginary animal from China which is shaped like a massive deer and has one or two horns and a fire-flame hide. The kirin is often represented in netsuke (see Plates 50 and 52); the true giraffe seldom. Material: boxwood. Signed: Shoko. Height: 4.1 cm. From Asahi Art, Tokyo.

PLATE 36. **DOG.** The dog in the illustration must be a favored pet, loved as much as a child, for it has a cushion on its back tied around with a sash. It may also be an allusion to the custom for pregnant women to wear maternity belts on the Day of the Dog in the hope of an easy birth, since dogs are known for their easy deliveries. In families where the old customs are still honored, a toy dog is often presented to a woman in labor as a prayer for an easy birth. Material: ivory. Unsigned. Height: 4.2 cm. From Tayama Art, Tokyo.

PLATE 37. **OX.** The artist designed the ox with the compactness of a good netsuke shape by turning the head back against the haunch. The piece is signed Tomotada. The first book on netsuke, the *Soken Kisho* published in 1781, describes Tomotada as famous for carving oxen and as having multitudinous imitators. Most Tomotadas are recumbent oxen of ivory, while the one illustrated is a standing ox of wood. Its age, design, and quality tend to confirm it as a true Tomotada. Material: wood. Signed: Tomotada. Height: 4.1 cm. From the collection of B. K. Denton, St. Louis.

PLATE 38. **BAKU.** The *baku* is an imaginary animal that performs a very charitable function: he eats bad dreams and nightmares. To secure his services it is necessary to write his name on a piece of paper and to sleep on it. Since the baku diets on rocks and iron, even the most terrible and revolting nightmares offer no difficulty to his digestive system, which far excels that of the python. Nevertheless, some dreams are so awful that the dreamer's best friends say that "even a baku would not eat *that* one."

The baku's nearest living relative is the tapir, a gentle beast but a nocturnal prowler, whose snout suggests half an elephant's trunk, just like the baku's. Material: wood. Unsigned. Height: 11 cm. From W. W. Winkworth, London.

PLATE 39. **SPARROW ON THE WING.** It is unusual to find the sparrow represented in flight. In paintings, it is sitting on a branch or walking on the ground. In netsuke, it is either a toy sparrow on wheels or a highly simplified and conventionalized design known as the inflated sparrow. The little bird suggests the popular children's fable, *The Tongue-Cut Sparrow,* which contains a moral about cruelty and greed.

The constant chattering of the sparrow gives rise to the popular expression, "talkative as a sparrow." Material: wood. Unsigned. Length: 5 cm. From the collection of Eizaburo Matsubara, Kyoto.

PLATE 40. **TOY TIGER.** Toy tigers made of heavy papier-mâché are popular gifts to children as expressions of the hope that they will be as strong and courageous as tigers. The type of toy tiger illustrated has a loose head so delicately balanced that the slightest current of air sets it in lifelike motion. The tail can be turned in any direction. Toy tigers range in size from miniscule to monsters larger than the child. Material: ivory. Signed: Hoichi. Length: 5.7 cm. From the collection of Frances Numano, Tokyo. For other Tigers, see Plates 41, 42, and 43.

PLATE 41. **STANDING TIGER.** The tiger is not indigenous to Japan, so Japanese artists had no experience with the animal in the flesh. The earliest representations were based on Chinese paintings and Buddhist images and ranged from oversized smiling house cats to fantastic beasts equal to the dragon in ferocity and strength.

Together the tiger and dragon are considered emblematic of the power of the Buddhist faith. The tiger is the greatest terrestrial power, the dragon the greatest celestial power. The breath of the tiger is wind, and the breath of the dragon is water. They are the irresistible force and immovable object of the East. Material: ivory. Signed: Hidemasa. Height: 4.5 cm. From Y. Tsuruki, Kyoto. For other Tigers, see Plates 40, 42, and 43.

PLATE 42. **CROUCHING TIGER.** In almost all representations the tiger is associated with the bamboo. This seems quite natural since the bamboo forest is the tiger's lair. However, Oriental philosophers see various meanings in the association:

Even the tiger, the strongest terrestrial animal, needs the assistance of the weak bamboo against the elements.

The tiger treading his way through poisonous jungle is the power of good over evil.

The protection given the tiger by the bamboo symbolizes the homage of the weak to the strong.

In the illustration, the artist has combined the tiger and bamboo by using bamboo for his material. Material: bamboo. Signed: 76-year-old Sekiran. Length: 4.3 cm. Illustrated in *The Art of the Netsuke Carver* (No. 92), by Frederick Meinertzhagen. For other Tigers, see Plates 40, 41, and 43.

PLATE 43. **DOLL TIGER.** Japanese dolls are not to be played with in the Western sense. Japanese dolls are assembled together and arranged as a sort of exhibit for visual enjoyment.

The doll illustrated is known as an Uji doll. This doll is made from the wood of the tea bush of the Uji district and in the style of carving first developed by Gyuka about 1840. The illustrated doll was carved by Gyuka's son, Kyusen Rakushiken. Material: tea-bush wood. Signed: Kyusen. Height: 5.1 cm. From the collection of Minagawa Seizan, Kyoto. For other Tigers, see Plates 40, 41, and 42.

PLATE 44. **WOMAN WRESTLER.** Professional Japanese wrestling *(sumo)* became very popular in the Tokugawa period. A related entertainment arose of wrestling between huge half-naked women sometimes selected as much for beauty as for physique. Soon entrepreneurs promoted wrestling matches between women and blind men who strangely groped for their female antagonists. The exhibitions became notoriously hilarious and lewd, and in 1872 wrestling between men and women was prohibited.

The characters on the woman's apron in the illustration read "Best in Japan." She certainly seems to be brimming with good health and *joie de vivre*. Material: wood. Signed: Ikkatsusai. Height: 8.6 cm. From Marcel Lorber, London. For another form of Wrestling, see Plate 93.

Plate 45. **PRIEST AND SCEPTER** (**NYOI**). The scepter *(nyoi)* is a ceremonial article held by a high-ranking Buddhist priest. The nyoi is usually in the design of the sacred mushroom of longevity. It is believed that with the power of the nyoi a high priest can grant any wish desired by the suppliant.

In the illustration, the priest uses the nyoi to scratch his back. The meaning is that it is easy to scratch another's back but very difficult to reach the itch on one's own, just as it is easy to give advice but difficult to solve one's own problems. Material: wood. Unsigned. Height: 7.1 cm. From the collection of Yonekichi Matsui, Osaka.

PLATE 46. **FOX-WITCH.** The fox dressed in the ancient court robes of a lady is an allusion to a case of royal fox-possession, the story of *Tamamo no Mae,* in which the fox-witch almost caused the slow death of the emperor by assuming the shape of a beautiful woman.

There are many tales of foxes assuming the shapes of beauties and ruining their pitiful mates with debauchery. Even today, a lovely temptress is called *kitsune* (fox). Material: ivory. Signed: Shiko. Height: 3.1 cm. From Takejiro Watanabe, Hiranoya, Tokyo. For other Foxes, see Plates 47 and 48.

PLATE 47. **FOX-PRIEST.** Japanese folklore is replete with fox-demons who assume various disguises, including human forms, causing sickness and even death. The fox-demon is the Oriental version of the legendary werewolf. The fox-demon is especially reprehensible when he assumes the form of a priest, as in the illustration, and hypocritically says his beads like the crafty beast he is. Material: wood, lacquer, and inlays. Signed: Kokoku. Height: 5.2 cm. From Marcel Lorber, London. For other Foxes, see Plates 46 and 48.

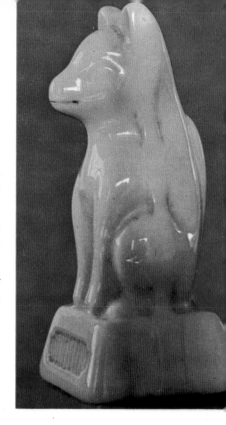

PLATE 48. **INARI FOX.** The Shinto shrines throughout Japan are devoted to various gods. Each god has a particular animal as his messenger. The Inari shrines are devoted to Inari, the God of Rice, who has as his messenger the fox. (This is a benign animal not to be confused with the demon-foxes of Plates 46 and 47.)

The Inari Fox of the illustration is not the one who stands guard at the entrance of the shrine but the cheap pottery fox sold as a souvenir of the shrine. The mould seam of the pottery is clearly simulated in the ivory. Material: ivory. Signed: Ishun. Height: 4.6 cm. Formerly in the collection of Wolf Ladejinsky. From Sotheby, London. For other Foxes, see Plates 46 and 47.

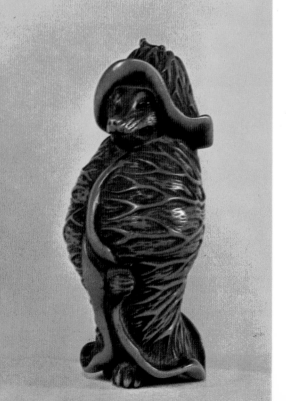

PLATE 49. **BADGER-PRIEST.** The badger often assumes human and other disguises, causing a lot of mischief with his pranks; but, unlike the fox, he is not malicious or evil. Everyone knows the badger is having fun because his bark sounds like laughter.

Sometimes the badger disguises himself as a priest and begs for religious contributions, really intending to fill the wine jug he carries on his back. Sometimes he beats his belly like a drum and and lures travelers into swamps—but this is just about his meanest trick. In the illustration, he has covered himself with lotus leaves, the sacred emblems of Buddhism, as though to make himself more Catholic than the pope, or rather, more Buddhist than the Buddha. Material: wood. Unsigned. Height: 5.3 cm. From the collection of Michael Braun, New York.

PLATE 50. **KIRIN (HAKUTAKU).** The *kirin* is the Oriental counterpart of the Occidental unicorn. However, while the horn of the unicorn precedes the animal, the horn of the kirin bends backward toward his neck. Despite this handicap, the kirin is quite the equal of the unicorn in auspicious portent. Its appearance marks the advent of a great and wise man, as witness the case of Confucius.

Kirin come in many species. The one illustrated talks. It is known, according to Joly's *Legend in Japanese Art,* as a *hakutaku.* Material: ivory. Unsigned. Height: 4.6 cm. From the collection of Zenshiro Horie, Nagoya. For another Kirin, see Plate 52.

PLATE 51. **SIAMESE CHESS HORSE.** The design is taken from the horse in the Siamese chess set. In Thailand the chess horse is quite conventionalized and invariably executed in ivory. The netsuke artist who was attracted by the design executed it in wood and colored it with lacquer, typical Japanese innovations. Material: wood. Unsigned. Height: 3.8 cm. From Hidezo Yagi, Kyoto. For other Foreign Designs, see Plates 24, 57, and 95.

PLATE 52. **KIRIN (KAIBUTSU).** The exact species of the kirin illustrated is difficult to determine. The Japanese collectors resort to a most convenient solution of such perplexing identification problems. *Kaibutsu* is a word which is a catch-all denoting all the fabulous and imaginary animals of land, sea, and air, of all the continents near and far, reported in both ancient and medieval Chinese chronicles and treatises. *This* kirin is therefore indubitably a *kaibutsu*. Material: staghorn. Unsigned. Height: 5 cm. From Peter Shimojo, Asahi Art, Tokyo. For another Kirin, see Plate 50.

PLATE 53. **SWIMMING SMELT.** Fish is preferred to meat by the vast majority of Japanese. The Japanese smelt rivals the shrimp in popularity as an ingredient of *tempura*. Material: mother-of-pearl. Unsigned. Length: 11.6 cm. From Nakabun, Tokyo. For other Fish, see Plates 54, 55, and 56.

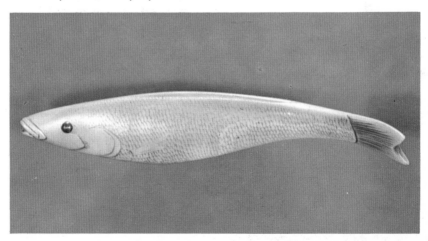

PLATE 54. **FARMERS' ART.** The fish illustrated is a product of what the Japanese call "farmers' art." By definition, the fish was carved by a man who made it for his own use or for a friend. It is the work of an amateur. While it is devoid of professional elegance, the design is spontaneous and primitive, rough and powerful. Material: wood. Unsigned. Length: 8 cm. From Shigeru Sawamura, Kyoto. For other Fish, see Plates 53, 55, and 56.

PLATE 55. **EARTHQUAKE FISH (NAMAZU).** In ancient times prior to the development of science, the terrible earthquakes that terrified and devastated Japan were attributed to the earthquake fish. This huge monster resides in the bowels of the earth from one end of Japan to the other. Whenever it wriggles, the earth above trembles and cracks. Material: ivory. Unsigned. Length: 7 cm. From Hideo Taniguchi, Kyoto. For other Fish, see Plates 53, 54, and 56.

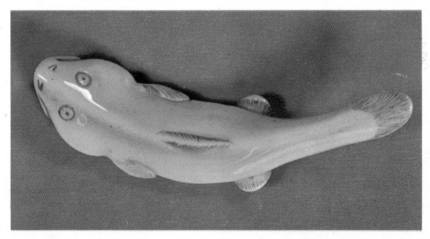

PLATE 56. **CARP (KOI).** The carp swims against the current, surmounting rapids and waterfalls. It is therefore the symbol of perseverance and manly courage.

The name for carp, *koi,* also means love. Traditionally, two carp portrayed together denote conjugal happiness. However, the disparity in age of the two carp illustrated leads one to hope that in this case the love is parental rather than conjugal. Material: wood. Signed: Masatoshi. Length: 6.5 cm. From Tatsuo Kubota, Shizuoka. For other Fish, see Plates 53, 54, and 55.

PLATE 57. **EUROPEAN INFLUENCE.** There is little doubt that the artist who carved this netsuke had a European model in mind. Quite likely, it was a cameo. Material: ivory. Unsigned. Length: 4.9 cm. From I. Asoh, Shinkoh-Shokai, Kobe. For other Foreign Designs, see Plates 24, 51, and 96.

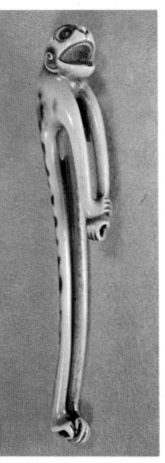
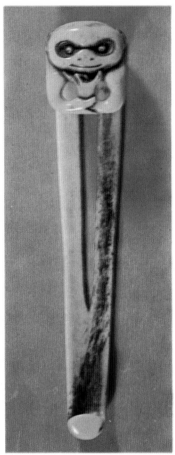
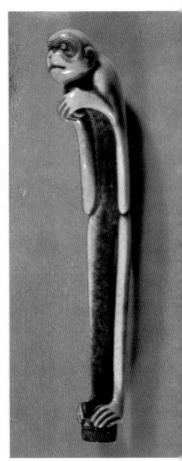

PLATE 58. **SASHI NETSUKE.** The three netsuke illustrated are a special elongated type worn thrust deep into the sash for support. They are called *sashi* netsuke.

All three were made by an artist named Kokusai. Kokusai had a sure feeling for the use of staghorn, his favorite material, and a keenly developed sense of whimsy. His carvings are marked with his originality and humor. His style is quite unmistakable.

Left: Material: staghorn. Signed: Koku(sai). Height: 12 cm. From K. Nagayama, Tokyo.

Center: Material: staghorn. Signed: Koku(sai). Height: 9.8 cm. From Niwa Curio, Tokyo.

Right: Material: staghorn. Signed: Koku(sai). Height: 10.6 cm. From Kazuo Itoh, Tokyo.

49

 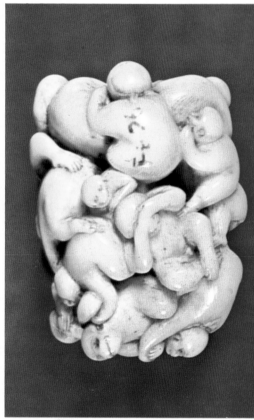

PLATE 59. **MONKEY GROUP.** Monkey Mountain at Beppu, a city on the Japan Sea, is a unique zoo with neither cages nor bars. It is a piece of level land with a small pond by which tourists congregate and buy peanuts. The monkeys—there are about 900—live in the mountains above. They are organized in groups with a big chief, sub-chiefs, and lookouts. When things get dull in the mountains, the monkeys, as by a signal, come down to the level land to look at the tourists and to feast on their peanuts.

There are always a few show-offs among the younger monkeys who climb trees and hurl themselves into the shallow pond. When their curiosity and appetites are satisfied, the monkeys troop back to the mountains without so much as a by-your-leave. Any youngster who tries to stay after the signal has been given can be sure of a cuff or a bite from a sub-chief.

The tourists look agape at the sudden departure and wonder whether it is they or the simians who are the sightseers. Material: ivory. Unsigned. Height: 4 cm. From Sotheby, London. For other Monkeys, see Plates 7 and 60.

PLATE 60. **MONKEYS AND LOQUATS.** Monkeys trained to do tricks are almost as old as history in Japan. In ancient times, trained monkeys wearing coats and hats entertained laborers working on imperial projects. The profession of monkey trainer *(sarumawashi)* has long been recognized.

The trainers with their performing monkeys were one of the few classes that were permitted to travel freely about the country. They had access to the territories and even to the residences of rival daimyos and were therefore ideal for spying. Many dramas and stories make use of this feature. Material: wood. Signed: Toyokazu. Width: 3.8 cm. From the collection of Hiroshi Takama, Gifu. For other Monkeys, see Plates 7 and 59.

PLATE 61. **KITE.** Kite flying is a favorite New Year's activity for boys and men. Some of the kites are huge, 30 or 40 feet in length, requiring dozens of hands to hold the cord. Japanese kites are in such various shapes as flags, birds, butterflies, actors, wrestlers, etc. and are decorated accordingly.

The kite illustrated is painted as a *yakko,* the low-class fellow who occupied the bottom rung of the feudal ladder. He was a servant and menial to the samurai and often took out his grievances by bullying the commoners. The commoners found revenge in making the yakko the butt of their ridicule and contempt. Material: lacquered wood. Unsigned. Width: 4.8 cm. From Tokuo Inami, Tokyo.

PLATE 62. **NARA DOLL.** Nara dolls are usually Noh actors carved in wood and painted in bright colors. The carving technique is always *ittobori,* sharp angular cutting to produce plane surfaces, and done with a single chisel.

Morikawa Toen (1820–1894) brought the Nara doll to a remarkable perfection. His work is preserved at the Tokyo National Museum and the Nara National Museum and is often exhibited.

Is Toen a genius? The Japanese critics rank him as one. They say he crossed the shadowy line that separates the artistic dollmaker from the master sculptor. Toen blended material, technique, and decoration in a perfect unison to express the stiff, angular, colorful brocade of the Noh costume. He instilled in his little figures an enchanting spirit of make-believe.

The Western collector has not yet "discovered" Toen. The reason may be the confusion caused by Toen's legions of copiers and imitators; it may be the psychological impact of the word "doll," which does not have the artistic connotation in the West that it enjoys in Japan; or it may be a failure to grasp a subtle Oriental appreciation. Material: painted wood. Signed: Toen. Height: 5.9 cm. From Jisaku Shimosaka, Yamanaka, Kyoto. Illustrated in the catalogue, "Exhibition of Morikawa Toen," (No. 62—Kasuga Dragon God Netsuke), held at the Nara National Museum, July 1943. For other Dolls, see Plates 43, 67, and 68.

PLATE 63. **RABBIT.** The rabbit's proud posture suggests a monarch and a throne. He is absolute ruler of the Year of the Rabbit.

The base on which he sits is an uncut seal. The 12 animals of the zodiac on individual seal bases were often made in China in jade or ivory. Frequently the bodies of the animals were human or half-human, the heads being those of the animals represented but with some distinctive feature grossly exaggerated or distorted, as for example the elongated ears of the rabbit illustrated. Material: ebony. Unsigned. Height: 4.3 cm. From S. Kawakatsu, Kyoto. For other Rabbits, see Plate 64.

PLATE 64. **RABBIT CIRCLE.** In the West we see the Man in the Moon, but in the East it is the Rabbit in the Moon. The circle formed by the three rabbits may, plausibly, represent the moon, but the Japanese collector sees a deeper significance.

He interprets the design as a modification of the three commas or comets *(magatama)* enclosed in a circle, the origin of which is buried in obscure Chinese metaphysics. It is the endless whirlpool of the heavens around the earth. It is the male and female principle *(yin* and *yang)* and the union of the two making the trinity. The three-comma design is often seen on the ends of tiles on temple roofs and in family crests *(mon)*. The illustration represents a substitution of rabbits for commas. It makes an auspicious netsuke for a man born in the Year of the Rabbit. Material: ivory. Unsigned. Diameter: 3.5 cm. From F. Kusaka, Shogado, Tokyo. For another Rabbit, see Plate 63.

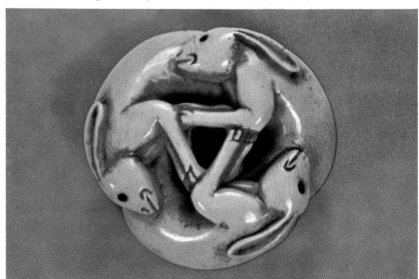

53

PLATE 65. **TOAD SENNIN.** *Sennin* are mountain hermits, or more picturesquely, "dwellers in the clouds." They are ascetics who develop supernatural powers through meditation and austerity. They live to an inordinate age while remaining joyous and youthful. Most sennin wear coats of leaves.

Sennin are usually identified by the animals or objects which are their attributes. The sennin most frequently portrayed in netsuke is the one associated with a toad. The toad is often the fanciful three-legged variety. Sometimes the Toad Sennin is as warty and ugly as his amphibious companion. Material: wood. Signed: Toyomasa. Height: 5.3 cm. From Soichi Kurono, Nagoya. For another Toad Sennin, see Plate 92. For other Sennin, see Plates 76 and 78.

PLATE 66. **WEASEL.** The weasel is called *kama-itachi* or sickle weasel on account of his sharp claws, which are like tiny scythes. Farmers say that by night he runs so quickly that he cannot be seen. Unaccountable scratches, including the romantic variety, are dismissed with the bland excuse that they were made by the invisible weasel. Material: ivory. Unsigned. Length: 4.2 cm. From Masayuki Odawara, Imperial Hotel Arcade, Tokyo. From the collection of Murray Sprung, New York.

PLATE 67. **RED LACQUER DOLL.** The doll illustrated is made of carved red lacquer *(tsuishu)*. As many as 200 or more coats of red lacquer are applied to a thin wood base. Each coat is individually dried and polished until a sufficient thickness is built. The design is then carved. The doll is the kind known as a *tachibina* or standing doll and is the female member of the pair represented in Plate 68. Material: red lacquer. Signed: Ho. Height: 4.4 cm. From Kazuo Itoh, Tokyo. For other Standing Dolls, see Plate 68. For other Dolls, see Plates 43 and 61.

PLATE 68. **STANDING DOLLS (TACHIBINA).** In former times, the Japanese family celebrated the Doll Festival with an outing. The girls of the family made crude paper dolls representing a man and a woman. The family carried the dolls to a river or stream and threw them into the water with the prayer that they carry away the family's sickness and misfortune. Later the crude paper dolls were made of stiffer material so that they would stand, and they were refined with the addition of clothes and decorations. The netsuke illustrates a familiar type of standing doll.

Today's Doll Festival is an elaborate display representing the life of the old imperial court. The dolls, numbering about 15, are all *seated*. They include the prince and princess, ladies in waiting, musicians, retainers, and guards. Fine old sets of dolls are often family heirlooms. Material: ivory. Signed: Rensai. Height: 3.4 cm. From Seijiro Yanagawa, Tokyo. For another Standing Doll, see Plate 67. For other Dolls, see Plates 43 and 61.

PLATE 69. **HAPPY CHINESE.** The Chinese laughs so hard that he must hold his head to keep it from bobbing. The reason for his joy is related in a Confucian anecdote. While the sage was traveling in Shantung Province, he met a very happy countryman and asked the reason for his happiness. The rustic answered:

"I distinguish clearly between good and evil; I pay my taxes; I honored my parents all their lives and, when they died, I buried them in accordance with the sacred rites. These are our most important duties. As I have performed them conscientiously and correctly, I am a happy man."

The Chinese thus stamped himself as a paragon of the social deportment and rectitude which are cornerstones of the Confucian ethic.

I am indebted to Mr. Sammy Yukuan Lee for the foregoing explanation. Material: wood. Unsigned. Height: 7.2 cm. From the collection of Sammy Yukuan Lee, Tokyo. For another Chinese, see Plate 88.

PLATE 70. **RYOMIN COPY OF SHUZAN.** This netsuke is signed "Ryomin copied Shuzan." Plate 20 illustrates the type of Shuzan that Ryomin copied. Shuzan's carving is bold, powerful sculpture. He used color to enhance his effects. On the other hand, Ryomin's style is delicate and elegant. He polished and finished his netsuke exquisitely. A comparison of the two netsuke leads to the inevitable conclusion that the extent of Ryomin's "copying" was actually only his use of a known Shuzan subject. Material: wood. Signed: Ryomin copied Shuzan. Height: 6.4 cm. From Mayuyama, Tokyo.

PLATE 71. **DOVE.** In the West the dove is the messenger of peace and good will, but in Japan she is the messenger of Hachiman, the God of War.

The grain of the carefully chosen wood emphasizes the toylike quality of the netsuke. The unknown artist simplified the design almost to the point of abstraction. Material: paulownia wood. Unsigned. Length: 5.5 cm. From Masao Hara, Tokyo.

PLATE 72. **SMIRKING OTAFUKU.** Uzume, Okame, Otafuku, and Ofuku are different names for the same woman, but just as her name undergoes transformations, so does her character. In the *Kojiki,* the earliest written Japanese records, she is Uzume, who performs a lewd and hilarious dance that sends the assembled progenitors of the Japanese race into gales of laughter. At village and shrine festivals she is Okame, with tiny features and pig eyes set in a fat round face, the personification of the ugly, good-natured woman.

As Otafuku or Ofuku she personifies hypocritical modesty and half-concealed eroticism. The illustrated netsuke is definitely Otafuku. Material: wood. Signed: Ikkansai. Height: 4.4 cm. From Kinsaburo Ueda, Toraya, Tokyo. For other representations of Okame, see Plates 73 and 74.

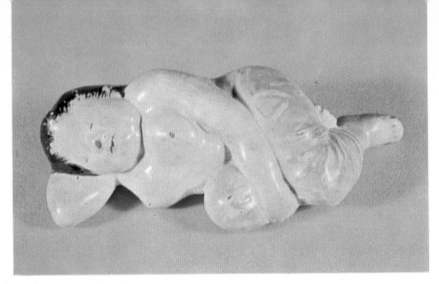

PLATE 73. **RESTING OKAME.** Occasionally one finds a carving that has the design, functionalism, and age associated with a good netsuke and yet does not fall into any of the styles, types, or categories found in netsuke illustrations and literature. Such a netsuke may be a rare find. It may be the work of an artist who was a modern in his own time, an artistic non-conformist who created by his own standards, disregarding popular preferences and rewards. A fine netsuke is all the more desirable if there is nothing quite like it. Material: painted wood. Signed: Sho. Length: 7.4 cm. From the collection of Mrs. Cherry Ishihara, Mikumo Prints, Kyoto. For other representations of Okame, see Plates 72 and 74.

PLATE 74. **POTTERY OKAME.** Miura Kenya (1825–1889) is a highly regarded ceramist who worked in the style of the earlier Kenzan and Ritsuo. The demand for netsuke grew to such large proportions in the 18th and 19th centuries that many potters, metal artists, mask carvers, and lacquerers fashioned netsuke as an adjunct to their main production. The illustration is an example of a netsuke made by a ceramist.

The fame of Ritsuo, Kenzan, and Kenya led to extensive forging of their signatures, but the fine quality of their work is not easily approached. Material: pottery. Signed: Kenya. Height: 3.9 cm. From the collection of Kenzo Imai, Kyoto. For other representations of Okame, see Plates 72 and 73.

PLATE 75. **SEIOBO SENNIN.** Among the 50 or so who attained the exalted rank of sennin in Buddhist and Taoist history, there has been only one woman. She is Seiobo. Her attribute is the peach. In her exotic gardens the peach blooms only once in 3,000 years, but the fortunate guest who partakes thereof acquires immortality.

The earliest carved netsuke were made in the Osaka area. A pronounced Chinese influence on them is clear. The subjects are mostly legendary people and animals, and the netsuke are unsigned, as is the practice in Chinese carving. The size is very large, in accord with the style then prevailing. The netsuke illustrated is an example of this early type. Material: ivory. Unsigned. Height: 10.7 cm. From Yamanaka, Kyoto. For other Sennin, see Plates 65, 78, and 92.

PLATE 76. **SIMPLIFIED CHILD.** This design is quite original and unique. The unknown artist drew heavily on his imagination to create a child with a style and character all its own. It is, therefore, difficult to assign the netsuke a particular classification by subject.

Perhaps the strongest influence discernible is that of the *gosho* doll, which is always a naked boy baby. The doll is covered with a fine oyster-shell powder, and absurdly tiny features are painted on a huge round head. The quality of the doll is the artless naïveté associated with a child. Material: wood. Unsigned. Height: 4.5 cm. From Yoshiaki Ohno, Tokyo.

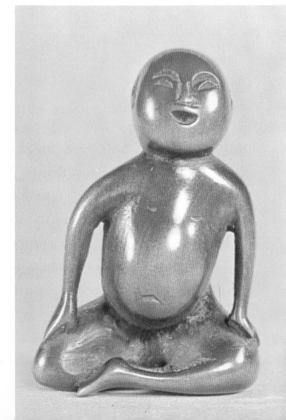

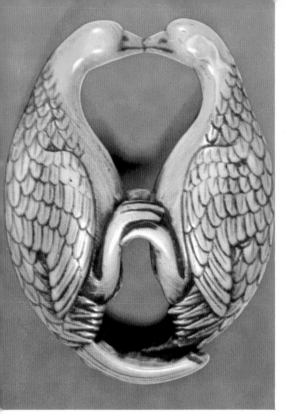

PLATE 77. **KISSING GEESE.** The design of the kissing geese illustrated was most certainly adopted from a family crest, or *mon*. The use of the mon in Japan is much wider than that of the heraldic coat-of-arms in Europe. Clubs, associations, professions, corporations, businesses, and shops, as well as families, have their mon. In this wider sense, mon is more accurately translated as "badge" than as "family crest." On formal occasions, Japanese often wear kimono designed with their family mon. Material: ivory. Unsigned. Height: 5.6 cm. From Giichiro Tahara, Miyanoshita, Hakone.

PLATE 78. **ONE-HORN SENNIN.** One-Horn Sennin was born of the marriage of his father with a deer; hence his horn. His father was also a sennin, but apparently found other diversions in the mountains besides ascetic contemplation.

One-Horn Sennin acquired great magical powers through a life of austere regimen and strict celibacy. However, one fateful day, he met a beautiful woman who had lost her way and become exhausted. He carried her pickaback as illustrated. Seeing her beautiful face reflected in the stream across which he waded and feeling her dear warmth, he experienced carnal sensations and desired earthly pleasures. Alas, poor One-Horn was instantly despoiled of his hard-earned merit and magical powers! Material: ivory. Signed: Hidemasa. Height: 5.8 cm. From Waju Kimura, Tokyo. For other Sennin, see Plates 65, 76, and 92.

PLATE 79. **SNAKE.** The Japanese language is rich in proverbs; they punctuate daily conversation. Snakes figure in many of the proverbs:

Instead of "Set a thief to catch a thief," the Japanese say "Set a snake to catch a snake"; instead of "Let sleeping dogs lie," the Japanese say "Poke a bamboo and start a snake." The Japanese equivalent of "Ignorance is bliss" is "Blind men fear not the snake"; the Japanese equivalent of "Once bitten, twice shy" is ;"The snake-bitten man fears a rope."

The meanings of many netsuke are obscure and difficult to elucidate. Sometimes the solution to the problem is discovered in a proverb. Material: wood. Signed: Sukenaga. Length: 3.6 cm. From Chozaburo Shimizu, Yokohama.

PLATE 80. **NARIHIRA.** *The Tales of Ise* (Ise Monogatari) is a 10th-century epic supposedly based on the amorous adventures of Narihira, the Japanese Casanova. Narihira was a man of fine appearance, royal birth, and great attainments. He was one of the Six Great Poets (Rokkasen) of 9th-century Japan.

The episode illustrated depicts Narihira abducting the beautiful Takako, who became the empress through a forced marriage. As a result of this adventure, Narihira was exiled. Material: ivory with lacquer design. Signed: Takahiro. Height: 3.6 cm. From the collection of Samuel Dubiner, Ramat Gam, Israel.

61

PLATE 81. **ASIATIC RAM.** The Chinese have used netsuke to support objects hung from the belt since ancient times. The Japanese borrowed the practice from the Chinese, but, starting with a simple article of utility, the Japanese impressed it with their artistic temperament and genius until they developed netsuke into an art form never envisioned by the Chinese originators.

The ram illustrated is an Asiatic fat-tailed sheep unknown in Japan. It is a *Chinese* netsuke made by a Chinese or Mongolian artisan for use on the Asiatic mainland. It should not be confused with foreign designs adopted by Japanese carvers such as those illustrated in Plates 24 and 51.

An almost identical ram is reproduced in *Substance and Symbol in Chinese Toggles* (No. 108), by Schuyler Cammann, who acquired it from a Mongol lama in the Ordos Desert, Mongolia. Material: prunus wood. Unsigned. Length: 5 cm. From Harishin, Kobe.

PLATE 82. **DEMON MASK.** There are about 100 masks used in the stately Noh drama and in the comic interludes called Kyogen. It is often difficult to identify the masks of Noh and Kyogen, as the variations are often very slight and the mask carvers exercised considerable license.

The Noh masks reveal a much more subtle art than do the ancient Greek masks with their static expressions of joy and sorrow. The Noh masks depict the *midway* emotion— the expression that is halfway between joy and sorrow, between hope and despair, between pride and modesty, etc. By tilting the mask at various angles and by adjusting his posture, the actor registers the emotion he wishes to convey. Material: wood. Unsigned. Height: 7 cm. From W. W. Winkworth, London.

PLATE 83. **FARMER.** The farmer rests a foot on his spade as he prepares to smoke his pipe for a moment of relaxation. He wears a makeshift straw coat *(mino)* as protection against the rain and straw sandals *(waraji)*. Material: wood. Signed: Gessen. Height: 6.4 cm. From Minoru Tanaka, Nagoya.

PLATE 84. **TAKANORI.** In the West, the warrior-poet seems almost a contradiction in terms. The Japanese, however, see no inconsistency in the general who writes poetry or the two-sworded samurai who swoons at the sight of cherry blossoms. Takanori is such a literary-military combination.

The emperor, though loyally supported by Takanori, is captured by the shogun and forcibly escorted into exile. In the illustration, Takanori writes a message of hope on a cherry tree in erudite characters which express subtle allusions. The meaning is beyond the capacity of the guards, but is clearly understood by the emperor. Material: ivory. Signed: Ikko. Height: 4.8 cm. From W. W. Winkworth, London.

PLATE 85. **HAWK.** The Oriental connoisseur considers economy of line in painting and economy of cut in sculpture as the hallmark of great art. The ideal is to express the most by the least. At the age of 80, Hokusai said that he would consider his career complete when he could convey strong emotion with a single sweep of his brush.

In the illustration, the unknown artist created a fine hawk's head from a natural bear's tooth with a minimum of carving. Material: bear tooth. Unsigned. Length: 7.3 cm. From Kuroda-ya, Osaka.

PLATE 86. **LIZARD.** Drugstores whose concoctions are based on the ancient Chinese pharmacopoeia *(kuroyaki-ya)* are still popular in Japan. The kuroyaki-ya dispenses animal hair, bones and teeth, the charred organs of snakes and other animals, and herbs. These unappetizing ingredients are ground and mixed into remedies for various complaints or into aphrodisiacs and potions. It is amusing to see a kuroyaki-ya side by side with a modern prescription pharmacy.

Occasionally one is surprised to hear an educated Oriental say that bile and blood from a live snake cured his stomach ailment where modern medicines had failed. However, some of the recipes of the kuroyaki-ya have been shown to contain in crude form the refined ingredient of the scientific drug.

The ashes of burnt lizard are considered a very potent love philter. (One wonders how the Japanese romantic persuades his love to swallow the revolting mess if she does not even like him to begin with.) The netsuke illustrated was probably worn as a charm to insure success in amorous undertakings. Material: wood. Unsigned. Length: 5.3 cm. From Masao Morita, Kyoto.

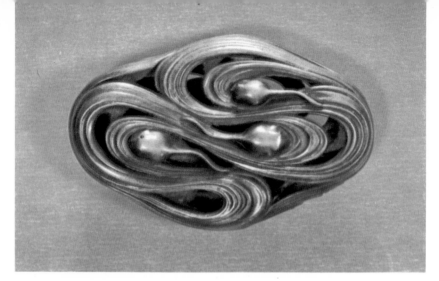

PLATE 87. **TADPOLES.** Toads and frogs are frequently represented in netsuke, but, unaccountably, the tadpole is extremely rare. The tadpoles of the illustration swim in a conventionalized stream. The type of netsuke is a *ryusa,* which means that the material is perforated clear through to make the design.

Japan has a great variety of frogs commonly called red, green, rain, and tree frogs, all of which croak as raucously as they do in other countries; but Japan is blessed with one extraordinary variety, the *kajika,* a tiny denizen of mountain streams that *sings* in a high sweet voice. The kajika is often kept as a pet, just as the singing cricket is. Material: wood. Signed: Soko. Length: 4.8 cm. From Shunichi Nishiura, Tokyo.

PLATE 88. **CHINESE SCHOLAR.** The demeanor and dress of the Chinese gentleman portrayed indicate that he is a scholar and official, commonly referred to as a mandarin. The mandarins were those who had passed competitive civil service examinations in the classics. As government officials, they were usually stationed in Peking. They did not represent a particular social class or a particular geographical area. The "Mandarin" dialect is the language spoken in the Peking area. Material: wood. Unsigned. Height: 12.5 cm. From W. W. Winkworth, London. For another Chinese, see Plate 69.

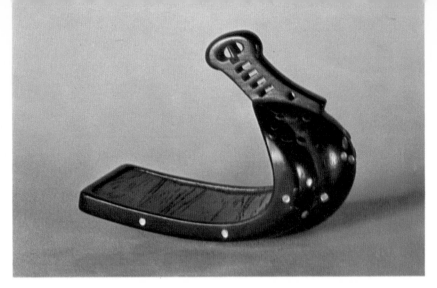

PLATE 89. **STIRRUP.** Old stirrups used by mounted samurai and by mounted priests in processions are beautiful objets d'art. The metal stirrups of the samurai are chased and inlaid; the lacquer ones of the priests are decorated in gold lacquer designs. A miniature replica, illustrated, serves as a netsuke.

Thousands of Japanese stirrups traveled abroad on the wave of a recent vogue in which they are used as flower stands. Material: light and dark wood with pearl inlays. Signed: Doraku. Length: 4.4 cm. From the collection of Alice Boney, Tokyo.

PLATE 90. **CHOHI.** Chohi was one of the three great warrior-heroes of China during the Han dynasty, along with Kan-u and Gentoku. Chohi is identified by his parted whiskers; Kan-u, by his long straight beard; and Gentoku, by his long arms that hang below his knees. Material: staghorn. Unsigned. Height: 8.8 cm. From Shoei Uchino, Heisando, Tokyo. For another representation of Chohi, see Plate 97.

PLATE 91. **RYUJIN.** Ryujin is the Dragon King who lives in a palace under the sea and rules the waves. He is the Neptune of the Orient. He is often represented wearing a dragon headdress and holding in his hands the jewel that controls the ebb and flow of the tides. Ryujin's assistants usually wear octopus headresses.

In the netsuke illustrated, the artist designed one assistant with his features twisted like the face of an octopus and the other with his features curled like the arms of an octopus. No one, neither god nor drunkard, is safe from the vagaries and humor of the netsuke artist. Material: wood. Unsigned. Height: 9.6 cm. From the Japan Art Center, Kyoto.

PLATE 92. **CORAL NETSUKE.** The tools and techniques employed in carving coral are quite different from those used in carving wood and ivory. Netsuke carvers had little experience with this material. It is, therefore, unusual to find a carved coral netsuke made prior to Meiji (1865), though polished red coral branches, uncarved and undecorated, occasionally served as netsuke. After Meiji, artisans began to work in coral.

The netsuke illustrated is an exception. It is a carved coral netsuke produced prior to Meiji. The subject is a Toad Sennin. Material: coral. Unsigned. Height: 5.1 cm. From K. Yokoyama, Kyoto. For another Toad Sennin, see Plate 65. For other Sennin, see Plates 76 and 78.

PLATE 93. **WRESTLING.** Many utterly ridiculous but hilarious forms of wrestling are depicted in Hokusai's *Manga* (Sketches), including the style illustrated. The wrestlers are pushing against each other with their behinds. They seem very intent on victory.

Hokusai's prolific and imaginative drawings furnished an almost inexhaustible fund of material for many of the netsuke artists. Material: painted wood. Signed: Nisai. Width: 4 cm. From the collection of Toshihiko Fujii, Nagoya. For a Woman Wrestler, see Plate 44.

PLATE 94. **DRAGONS.** There are five intertwined dragons in this little bit of sculpture, all with heads, tails, horns, legs, and claws. Despite the host of appendages, despite the writhing of the serpents, despite the awkward accessibility for carving, and despite a most complicated design, all parts fall neatly and elegantly in place.

The mechanical problem facing the artist when he first put knife to ivory and the final results are all the more remarkable when we remember that most netsuke carvers did not make practice models or even preliminary sketches. They believed that to do so would dissipate their artistic energy and power. The carver conceived the design only in his mind's eye. When satisfied, he immediately cut into his material. Material: ivory. Signed: Ikkosai. Length: 4.5 cm. Illustrated in *The Art of the Netsuke Carver* (No. 98), by Frederick Meinertzhagen.

PLATE 95. **CHINESE GONG.** The model for the illustrated netsuke is an ancient Chinese gong and stand kept at the Shoso-in, the Imperial Treasure House in Nara. The Shoso-in contains a great variety of precious art of Chinese origin collected during the 8th and 9th centuries A.D.

There are many collections of rare Chinese art in Japan. These collections have led to the observation that the Chinese created the art, but the Japanese preserved it. Material: wood. Unsigned. Height: 8.3 cm. From Sotoo Nagano, Tokyo. For other Foreign Designs, see Plates 24, 51, and 57.

PLATE 96. **DONKEY AND GROOM.** A wonderful aspect of netsuke has nothing to do with their intrinsic value as art. Netsuke tell a great deal about the social life of the common man that is not found in the pages of history. Did he play the *koto*, tell a funny story, imitate a crane, laugh at a woman in her tub, run from thunder, or wipe a donkey's hoof as in the illustration? All is told in netsuke. Netsuke are a mirror of the beliefs and activities of the Japanese during the last three centuries. Material: wood. Unsigned. Width: 5 cm. From Yasushi Ouchi, Tokyo.

PLATE 97. **CHOHI MOUNTED.** The netsuke purist will disqualify the illustration as not a "true" netsuke. For him, the carving is too intricate, delicate, and pointed. His test is whether there is a smooth, rounded feeling in the palm of his hand when the netsuke is held. Nevertheless, many carvings of the type illustrated were made expressly for Tokyo and Osaka merchants who had grown rich in the new foreign trade. These netsuke were worn, albeit most gingerly, for vanity and show.

Conceding that such carvings do not qualify as "true" netsuke raises a larger question: Do they qualify as sculpture? Material: ivory. Signed: Masatsugu. Height: 4.9 cm. From Yuki Nakai, Tokyo. For another representation of Chohi, see Plate 90.

PLATE 98. **MASSAGE.** In the West, the purpose of massage is therapeutic, but in Japan the purpose is to gain a feeling of well-being. Massage is widely practiced in Japan, particularly at hot-spring resorts, where the keynote is relaxation. During the Tokugawa period, massage was encouraged, and schools of various techniques developed. The profession of masseur *(amma)* was restricted to the blind. Even today a large percentage of the amma are blind.

The netsuke carver delighted in portraying a man receiving the rough handling from the amma that produces the expression of "an agony of pleasure," as in the illustration. Material: wood with lacquered parts. Signed: Seisho. Width: 4.5 cm. From Kawabun, Kyoto.

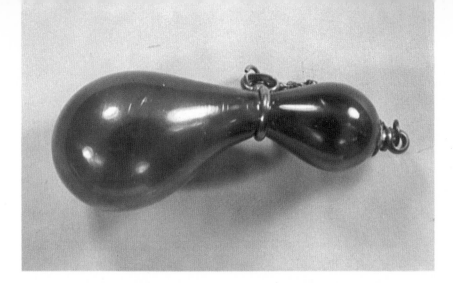

PLATE 99. **SATSUMA GLASS.** The old Satsuma pottery and porcelain of Kagoshima is world-renowned. While Satsuma glass is less well known, its quality is equally superb.

The narrow-waisted gourd *(hyotan)*, with its endless variations of form and shape, was used in its natural state as a netsuke long before the innovation of carving and decoration. So attractive do the Japanese find the hyotan that artisans copied the natural object in all the numerous materials found in netsuke. Nevertheless, netsuke of Satsuma glass are quite rare. Material: glass. Unsigned. Length: 6.9 cm. From Y. Tsuruki, Kyoto.

PLATE 100. **LION (SHISHI).** *Shishi* are also called Chinese lions *(kara-shishi)* and Korean dogs *(koma-inu)*. The shishi is the commonest subject in netsuke, and the varieties are endless. Despite the name and the abundance, one never sees a shishi that could pass for a lion. This fact substantiates the advice of the ancient Chinese artist to his pupils: "Draw swans, but not lions. Your swans may at least look like ducks, but your lions will only look like dogs." Material: wood thinly coated with red lacquer. Unsigned. Length: 3.9 cm. From Junzo Niimi, Tokyo.